TO JUNE AND BUZZ,

There's a song by Celine Dion that echoes in my heart every time I think of you. It's more than just lyrics; it's a testament to your love, a love that has been my strength, my voice, my eyes:

"You were my strength when I was weak
You were my voice when I couldn't speak
You were my eyes when I couldn't see
You saw the best there was in me
Lifted me up when I couldn't reach
You gave me faith 'cause you believed
I'm everything I am
Because you loved me"

- Celine Dion, Because You Loved Me

Whispers of Hope: Poetic Reflections on Family and Life

Whispers of Hope: Poetic Reflections on Family and Life

Liam Sawyer

Published in the United States by Liam Sawyer
an imprint of Sawyer Original.
New York, NY

Author: Liam Sawyer

First Edition: Dec 1, 2023

ISBN: 979-8-9890576-0-3 (Softcover)
ISBN: 979-8-9890576-1-0 (Hardcover)
ISBN: 979-8-9890576-2-7 (ePub Edition)

Library of Congress Control Number: 2023916393

"Whispers of Hope: Poetic Reflections on Family and Life" is a stand-alone collection but it carries the emotional legacy of my original memoir, *"Wishes of Love"*. It's a poetic exploration of life, love, and loss, inspired by personal experiences and observations.

For permissions, please contact:
Liam Sawyer
Website: *liamsawyer.com*

To everyone who has walked with me on this journey, thank you for being part of my story. Together, we continue to whisper hope into the world.

CONTENTS

PART I

DAWN OF A NEW LIFE

PART II

SHADOWS AND ECHOES

PREFACE

Life is a mosaic of moments, a tapestry woven with threads of memories, emotions, and experiences. Each of us carries a unique story, one that is shaped by the choices we make, the challenges we face, and the love we give and receive. This book is a reflection of my journey, a collection of poems that encapsulate the essence of my memoir, "Wishes of Love."

While my memoir delved deep into the narrative of my life, this book offers a different perspective. It presents distilled moments, thoughts, and feelings that have shaped my existence. From the streets of Ukraine to the bustling life of New York City, from the depths of despair to the heights of joy, these poems capture the essence of my experiences.

As you flip through these pages, you may find a poem that resonates with your own journey, or you might be transported into a world different from your own.

Either way, my hope is that these words inspire reflection, evoke emotions, and remind you of the power of love, hope, and family.

This book is not just a collection of poems; it's a testament to the resilience of the human spirit, the importance of identity, and the unbreakable bonds of family. Whether you've read my memoir or are discovering my story for the first time, I invite you to journey with me once again, this time through the lens of poignant poems that have defined my life.

Thank you for being a part of this journey.

PART I: DAWN OF A NEW LIFE

BEGINNINGS

TAKE ME AWAY

In childhood's gentle embrace we stood,
Blind to the ease others understood.
I thought all lived as I once did,
Innocence hid what life's curtains hid.
All hearts, I believed, beat just like mine.

The youngest, I sought treasures unseen,
In the forest's embrace, so lush and green,
Unaware of the world, vast and untamed, beyond my
dream.

In the corridor where echoes play,
Eyes filled with wonder, watch my way.
Each gaze a story, a silent praise,
With hope that in their depths does blaze,
A dance of dreams that never sway.

Every knock upon the door,
Every footstep on the floor,
Held a silent, hopeful beat,
A yearning heart, a wish so sweet,
That maybe, just maybe once more,
They'd return, as they did before.

My sister, strong amid the tide,
In uncertain worlds, by my side,
A guardian where shadows hide.

In the void where parents once stood,
Siblings rise, doing all that they could,
An anchor in life's shifting wood.
Protectors in every misunderstood,
Guides through both bad and good,
Their love, deeper than any childhood,
A bond, unbreakable, always understood,
A promise, a pact, forever withstood.

In the orphanage, with walls so gray,
Hope's bright light starts to fray,
Each passing day, a slow decay,
Yet in silent hearts, dreams still sway.

New walls, new voices, echoing above,
Different settings, but one constant shove,
That hope, that wish, like a homing dove,
To belong, to be cradled, to be loved.

Days blend with hope unchanged.

In Ukraine's depths, where winters bite,
In an orphanage, dimly lit, not quite right,
Children lay dreaming, every cold night,
Of a door opening, of a future bright.

The icy winds told tales of plight,
But in their hearts, a flame did ignite,
Each hoping to be the one in sight,
When visitors came, searching for light.

A single glance, a promise, a kite,
Could lift them from depths to a height,
Away from the cold, away from the fight,
Into arms warm, where love would alight.

Though they stood together, each had a rite,
To hope, to dream, to take their flight,
Away from the chill, into the warm light,
Wishing to be chosen, every single night.

DISCOVERIES
THE FOREIGN VISITORS

In a child's gaze, each face,
A promise, a future's embrace,
A new beginning, a hopeful grace.

Hope is a smile that spreads,
A radiant glow that treads,
Even in the unknown's threads,
Cheek to cheek, no fear it dreads,
Guiding us where the heart leads,
A beacon that forever heeds,
In darkness, in doubt, it feeds,
Our strength, our dreams, our deeds.

Eyes as blue as sky's embrace,
Voices like home, a familiar place,
On a sunny day, they grace,
A warmth, a comfort, a loving trace.

In a world of faces unknown,
Where connections are rarely shown,
It's the heart's warmth, brightly blown,
That stands out in a crowd, alone.

A smile, a glance, a gentle tone,
Becomes a beacon, a heartfelt zone,
A symbol of kindness, all our own,
An impression lasting, forever sewn.

Bubbles rise, simple yet profound,
Magic floating, joy unbound,
Hours pass, laughter surrounds,
In simplicity, true delight is found.

For a child's heart, vast and round,
A bubble machine, where dreams are crowned,
Glimmering orbs, to the sky they're bound,
Gateway to wonder, where happiness is unconfined.

Gifts of fruit, toys in procession,
Yet above all, time's warm concession,
Their affection, trust's true expression,
Becomes the greatest, most cherished lesson.

In the vastness where shadows reside,
Where uncertainty and fears coincide,
Though you loom, vast and wide,
I stand strong, unwavered, by the side.

For every doubt, for every space,
For every question, every chase,
I offer solace, a warm embrace,
A beacon, a light, in this vast maze.

Know that with every daunting phase,
My strength will always erase,
Your fears, with love's tender grace.

-Hope

A new name, whispers of destiny,
A fresh start, where love's the remedy,
With a family that chose, setting us free,
A new identity, where hearts agree.

In the act of renaming, see,
A commitment, a bond, a decree,
A promise that echoes, vibrant and key,
Of belonging, of roots, like a sturdy tree.

A future painted with love's spree,
Embraces, laughter, and endless glee,
Where every moment's a jubilee,
In the dance of love, forever we'll be.

Blizzards rage, the world outside,
Inside, storms of doubt reside.

Even after a brief parting tide,
The joy of reunion can't be denied.
A testament, deep and wide,
To bonds forming, side by side.

Every embrace, every stride,
Speaks of love, amplified.
The warmth, the trust, the pride,
In this dance, love is our guide.

THIS NEW LIFE

Every step away, a daunting trace,
From the familiar, the known embrace,
Yet with courage, we face the space,
A leap towards life, a new pace.

Each footfall, a path we chase,
Towards dreams, a vibrant race,
A new life, a freshened grace,
Our future's call, we warmly face.

In a child's heart, pure and tender,
Every new sight, a magical splendor,
A wonder bright, an enchanting sender,
Every new sound, a melodious defender,
A symphony of life, sweet and slender,
A melody of joy, a heart's surrender.

In a world of unknowns, a vast array,
Touch becomes the guide, a tactile play,
The language of exploration, a new way,
Curiosity's path, a discovery's sway,
Unfolding mysteries, day by day.

The thrill of flight, wings taking hold,
The magic of screens, stories unfold,
The joy of new words, treasures untold,
A world awakened, brave and bold.

In the glow of a sunset, a child stands tall,
Whispers to the wind, tales of a journey, a thrall,
"Mama, America good," words pure, without a stall,
The realization of dreams, a hope that won't fall.

Through hardships and storms, past every wall,
Seeking refuge, hearing freedom's call,
The words of a heart, echoing in the hall,
Finding its new home, amidst it all.

With gratitude profound, tears might befall,
But the heart knows, it's found its protocol,
In the land of dreams, where possibilities sprawl,
The child's words, a testament, enthral.

Embracing the warmth, of love's protocol,
With each day, new horizons install,
Grateful for the embrace, for breaking the thrall,
For in these words, love's truth does enthrall.

Every bite, a journey unknown,
Of unfamiliar food, seeds of curiosity sown,
A taste of the world, in flavors shown,
Waiting to be explored, a vastness grown.

With every morsel, horizons are flown,
Realizations dawn, as senses hone,
A vast world out there, yet to be known,
Gratitude in discovery, in every tone.

A world in a bite, a map overthrown,
New experiences, new cultures, a zone,
Where the heart finds joy, fully blown,
Tasting the vastness, the world has shown.

In every stumble, a lesson clear,
In every fall, a story near,
A dance with life, a tango with fear,
An embrace of growth, ever dear.

Adaptation's song, a constant cheer,
Challenges faced, with a pioneer's spear,
A journey of growth, year by year,
Embracing the falls, with a smile sincere.

Even stairs become mountains high,
Challenges looming, reaching the sky,
When you've never climbed, never did try,
They stand as tests, under life's watchful eye.

A lesson in patience, a call to comply,
Adaptation's dance, never awry,
Embrace the climb, let fears untie,
Scale those mountains, let your spirits fly.

In the vast expanse of space and time,
The brightest lights often silently chime,
Not in rooms, where shadows depart,
But deep within, warming a heart.
Guiding, embracing, like an art,
Their radiant glow, a love's chart,
Kindling souls, right from the start.

"Welcome Home," two words so slight,
Yet they carry a universe, pure and bright,
Echoing promises, holding tight,
A beacon of belonging, hearts alight,
In their embrace, everything feels right.

Neighbors become friends, the first embrace,
Friends become family, a loving chase,
A house shifts, a transformation's grace,
Becomes a home, a heartfelt place.

Bonds grow strong, connections trace,
A dance of love, a warm interface,
Community thrives, in every face,
A world united, a beautiful base,
Together we stand, in love's endless space.

In the heart of a new land, vast and free,
The sweetest taste, beyond sights to see,
Is not of food, but of bonds that be,
The warmth of community, a heart's decree,
A connection profound, a unity's plea,
A love that thrives, an endless spree.

PART II: SHADOWS AND ECHOES

MEMORIES
ORPHANAGE OR SCHOOL?

From flashcards to schoolyards, a journey unfolds,
Every word, a key, every letter, a mold,
A step towards understanding, a path to behold,
A new world, vibrant, stories untold.

Through learning and growth, dreams take flight,
Words become wings, days turn bright,
Embracing the challenge, with all our might,
Understanding blossoms, a welcomed sight,
In the dance of language, a pure delight,
A world connected, in wisdom's light.

In the eyes of a child, so clear and wide,
Every building stands tall, secrets inside,
A universe waiting, with doors open wide,
To be explored, no mysteries to hide.

Walls whisper stories, windows invite,
A world of wonder, an explorer's delight,
Growth through discovery, an endless flight,
In every corner, learning takes its right.

Echoes of past, haunting the mind,
Goodbyes that were, memories unkind,
A school bell rings, but what does it find?
A siren of abandonment, fears intertwined.

Past shadows loom, hard to leave behind,
Each chime, a memory, hard to unbind,
Yet in the echo, hope we can find,
A chance for healing, for hearts to rewind.

To trust anew, to redefine,
The sounds of the world, in a positive line,
For amidst the fears, strength is designed,
Facing the past, letting trust shine.

In the heart of a child, so raw and pure,
Every separation, an uncertain detour,
A test of trust, a challenge to endure,
Fear of the unknown, hard to ignore.

Yet with every test, trust grows more sure,
Bridges of belief, built to assure,
In the dance of love, bonds secure.

Amidst the chaos, when the world appears unclear,
When emotions surge, and eyes fill with tears,
In the stormiest moments, when the heart fears,
The sight of a familiar home, to us it steers.

A beacon of solace, in life's vast frontier,
A place of refuge, where memories adhere,
Its walls whisper tales, its warmth sincere,
Calming the tempest, making the path clear.

For home is more, than bricks or veneer,
It's where comfort lives, where loved ones are near,
A sanctuary of assurance, year after year,
The heart knows it's safe, nothing left to fear.

For in its embrace, everything is dear,
The stormiest of tears, quickly disappear.

Sometimes, the world feels cold and apart,
Doubts arise, shadows cloud the heart,
But the promise of a meal, a simple start,
Bridges the gap, like a work of art.

Between fear and comfort, a delicate chart,
A gesture of kindness, a love to impart,
For food is more than taste, it's a magic dart,
That mends broken spirits, makes sadness depart.

In every bite, assurance takes part,
Binding souls together, a union to kickstart.

To a heart that's known loss, tender and bruised,
Every goodbye echoes, memories fused,
Of past separations, scars never excused,
A haunting reminder, emotions confused,
Yet strength emerges, resilience used,
Facing the echoes, past pain refused.

In the shadow of past traumas, a haunting shade,
Perceptions altered, innocence begins to fade,
Even a school, a place of learning and trade,
Can look like an orphanage, memories replayed.

Walls no longer vibrant, but cold and dismayed,
A place once joyful, now carries a blade,
Yet within the heart, courage must be weighed,
To see beyond shadows, fears allayed.

For in the eyes of understanding, love won't evade,
Healing will come, new bonds will be made,
In the embrace of compassion, memories will fade,
A school will be a school, fears will degrade,
The orphanage image, in trust's light, will cascade.

A parent's presence, profound and true,
Even from afar, in skies of blue,
Radiates love, a color so new,
A beacon of security, breaking through.

In a child's world, where dreams accrue,
Storms may rage, and fears may brew,
Yet with their light, hope is renewed,
Guiding, comforting, like morning dew,
An everlasting bond, forever to glue.

In the vastness of life, among stars above,
There's a promise, gentle as a dove,
Of a waiting home, a treasure trove,
Filled with memories, and stories wove.

The assurance of a parent's love, a protective glove,
A constant embrace, push comes to shove,
With every heartbeat, dreams thereof,
Their love's a guide, when things get tough.

In their promise, all fears dissolve,
Their love's an enigma, forever to solve,
An eternal dance, endlessly to evolve.

From the cries, raw and profound,
Uncertainty's echoes, an overwhelming sound,
Yet with time, on this new ground,
Children find their way, safe and sound.
From despair's lows to recess's high,
Adapting, growing, reaching for the sky,
With resilience, their spirits never shy.

In the heart of a child, vibrant and untamed,
Every challenge faced, a fire unflamed,
An adventure waiting, a destiny unnamed,
Hurdles arise, yet spirits unmaimed.

For every test, every twist and turn,
Is but a game, a lesson to learn,
With laughter and tears, their spirits churn,
Facing the unknown, at every concern.

Yet, with brave hearts, they discern,
That every challenge can be overturned,
With resilience, victory is earned,
And in their joy, the world is turned.

HEARTACHES
LOSS OF LOVE

In the open field, under the sun's golden wand,
The sound of a bat, a connection so fond,
The ball soars high, over the pond,
A father and son, of each other so fond.

The cheers, the roars, in this sacred bond,
Stories told, lessons dawned,
In the joy of a game, they respond,
Echoes of love, far beyond.

Every pitch, every stance,
Every moment, every chance,
Together they dance, in life's vast expanse,
Their bond growing, with each passing glance,
In the rhythm of the game, in love's true romance.

In the canvas of life, with colors so free,
The simplest moments, stand out with glee,
A shared treat, under a shade tree,
Becomes a memory, as vast as the sea.

A laugh, a smile, a playful decree,
The taste of joy, pure and spree,
Cherished memories, as sweet as honeybee,
In the heart they reside, forever to be.

It's not about grandeur, or a spending spree,
But the warmth, the bond, the unity,
Moments so fleeting, yet they decree,
The depth of love, and its continuity.

Holding close, in times of glee and decree,
Such moments become, life's true decree.

In an instant, time's fickle hand,
Can twist the joy, into a strand,
Of heartbreak so severe, so unplanned,
The world can shift, like desert sand.

Laughter turns to tears, dreams to despair,
The colors fade, the sky seems unfair,
A moment's change, an unwelcome glare,
Leaves the soul bare, in sorrow's lair.

Yet in the darkness, we must find the light,
Hold on to memories, with all our might,
For love endures, beyond the darkest night,
In hearts, it glows, forever bright.

Even in loss, it's our guiding kite,
Leading us through, to hope's new height.

The weight of silence, heavy and profound,
After a loved one's voice, no longer resounds,
Is immeasurable, a void so confound,
A haunting emptiness, all around.

A voice once lively, full of zest,
Now quiet, leaves the heart oppressed,
Memories echo, in the chest,
A longing, a craving, a relentless quest.

Yet in the silence, if we dare to hear,
Their whispers linger, close and near,
In every breeze, every tear,
A reminder, they're always here.

In love's embrace, we persevere,
Through loss, through pain, year after year,
With courage and faith, we steer,
Holding dear, those who were near.

For the silence speaks, if we adhere,
Love's eternal song, forever clear.

The hardest goodbyes, sharp and sudden,
Are the ones, by surprise they're ridden,
We never saw coming, no forewarning given,
Leaving hearts wounded, souls heavily laden.

Moments before, laughter and song,
In a heartbeat, all feels wrong,
The world's vibrant hues, no longer strong,
A lingering echo, a grief prolonged.

Yet in this pain, realizations awake,
Cherishing moments, for memory's sake,
Holding close, every handshake, every heartbreak,
Understanding life's fragility, with every breath we
take.

In the eyes of a child, pure and wide,
The absence of a parent, cannot hide,
An endless void, a gaping tide,
A longing, a craving, deep inside.

Every laugh, every stride,
Feels empty, without them by the side,
The world feels vast, an endless ride,
Yet in their heart, the void won't subside.

Questions arise, emotions collide,
Why did they leave? Why did they bide?
Yet, amidst the tears, love won't hide,
Memories of warmth, forever tied.

With time and love, wounds will slide,
Yet the love remains, forever amplified,
In the heart's chambers, love will reside.

The true measure, not in years or gold,
Is found in stories, heartwarmingly told,
By those left behind, with memories to hold,
Of love and lessons, courageously bold.

It's not the fame, nor grandeur amassed,
But the impact made, the shadow cast,
On hearts and souls, in memories vast,
A legacy, in time, unsurpassed.

Every smile shared, every hand lent,
Moments of grace, times well spent,
Laughter, tears, the messages sent,
These are the measures, of life's event.

In tales of kindness, love unconfined,
Lies the true measure, of a life, defined.

In the tapestry of life, vast and stark,
Some souls stand out, leaving an indelible mark,
Brief encounters, yet they spark,
A light, a flame, in the heart's dark.

A fleeting moment, a brief glance,
Yet their essence, leaves a lasting trance,
In memories they dance, given a chance,
Their spirit alive, in life's vast expanse.

Even if time, quickly parts,
Their legacy lingers, in many hearts,
For the depth they bring, forever imparts,
An indelible mark, in life's many arts.

At seven, with eyes wide and pure,
The world is simple, that's for sure,
Laughter and play, life's allure,
But the pain of loss, there's no cure.

Complexity of grief, deep and vast,
An emotion so big, shadows cast,
Over a heart so young, contrasts,
With the simplicity, of the past.

Yet, within this tender age,
The strength to cope, takes center stage,
Understanding grows, page by page,
Embracing pain, the heart's sage.

Loss knows no age, it's true,
But resilience in youth, continues to renew.

In the dance of life, moments are brief,
Time with loved ones, joy and grief,
Yet, even if it's fleeting, like a falling leaf,
Their impact is lasting, beyond belief.

A smile, a touch, a shared belief,
Moments so short, yet they bequeath,
Lessons and memories, love's motif,
An everlasting bond, underneath.

Their voices echo, their laughter chimes,
Resonating through, life's climbs,
While the clock counts, in fleeting times,
Their legacy lasts, in heart's rhymes.

For love's impact, knows no confines.

In life's vast theater, on the grand stage,
Unpredictability plays, age to age.
With every sunrise, every turn of the page,
Life writes tales, both calm and rage.

Moments of joy, and sudden despair,
Laughter today, tomorrow's tear,
Life's unpredictability, beyond compare,
It's the constant, in the changing air.

Yet within its fragile, fleeting state,
Are lessons profound, a twist of fate.
For amidst its uncertainty, life does state,
The beauty of now, before it's too late.

Embrace every moment, every trait,
For life's unpredictability, we can't negate.
It's the most certain dance, in our date,
Teaching us to love, before the closing gate.

In the dance of life and death,
every moment is a step,
every memory a song.

GROWING UP
RESPONSIBILITIES

In life's grand play, roles sometimes shift,
With twists and turns, and the tectonic drift.
In the absence of one, the void is vast,
Yet, from the shadows, a hero is cast.

Not always the strongest, or the most wise,
But the one who sees, through the disguise,
Of fear and doubt, and the overwhelming size,
Of the challenge ahead, and the prize.

For when one falls, or takes a step back,
Another must rise, filling the lack.
With courage and heart, on the winding track,
They step up, carrying the pack.

A beacon of hope, a guiding light,
Showing the way, through the darkest night.

The weight of the world, sometimes bends,
The mantle of responsibility, it sends.
Not always to the eldest, or the one with years,
But often to the youngest, amidst their tears.

Young shoulders, sturdy and strong,
Step up to the plate, righting the wrong.
Guided by love, and the need to belong,
They wear the mantle, singing life's song.

With every challenge, every boulder,
The youngest grow wiser, and much older.
For in their hearts, and their holder,
Rests the strength, of the world's beholder.

Holidays come, with festive cheer,
Yet the void is felt, year after year.
Tables adorned, with dishes vast,
But empty chairs remind, of the past.

Rooms filled with echoes, of laughter once shared,
Memories of moments, when everyone cared.
The tinkle of bells, the festive song,
Yet something feels missing, something feels wrong.

The joy of the season, a bittersweet taste,
For loved ones absent, can't be replaced.
Yet in the silence, if we listen close,
Their love still lingers, their spirit engross.

While holidays change, without them around,
In memories, their laughter and love still sound.

In the wake of loss, the world turns gray,
Even the brightest days, lose their ray.
Sunshine feels cold, nights longer still,
Shadows of grief, over the windowsill.

Yet within the dim, a faint light glows,
A remembrance of love, that never goes.
The warmth once shared, the bond so tight,
In memories, breaks through the night.

Though days may feel dim, and nights so long,
The love once shared, remains ever strong.
For in the heart's shadow, love does cling,
A beacon of hope, making the soul sing.

Even in loss, love remains the theme,
Guiding the heart, in its dream.

In the grand tapestry of life, threads intertwine,
Family and friends, together they shine.
Yet often, in the quietest corner, there's a gleam,
From a source unexpected, a subtle beam.

Not the loudest voice, or the tallest tree,
But a silent supporter, as strong as can be.
Sometimes, the unassuming, the ones we neglect,
Become our pillars, with the strongest effect.

When storms rage and winds blow,
These pillars stand, in the shadowed glow.
Holding us firm, when the world's in defect,
Their strength and love, we come to respect.

For life teaches, in its intricate art,
The most unexpected, hold the strongest heart.

In the vastness of life, moments come and go,
Yet in absence, emotions deeply flow.
The quiet of a room, the unsaid goodbye,
Makes the heart wail, its loudest cry.

Empty chairs, silent phones, vacant halls,
Echo the love that forever calls.
For in the void, the heart feels most,
The warmth of memories, like a ghost.

Yet, amidst the silence, love does speak,
Whispering tales, every day, every week.
For even in absence, love doesn't die,
It's the heart's eternal lullaby.

From the bustling streets, to quiet home lanes,
A mother's journey, is one of gains.
Through the maze of life, she steadily paves,
A path of dreams, on which love waves.

From tiny shoes, to graduation caps,
Her love is the map, bridging the gaps.
In the heart of the city, or in silent nooks,
Her love is the foundation, upon which life looks.

Each lesson taught, each tear wiped away,
Is a step on the journey, a sunray in the gray.
For in every challenge, and every strive,
A mother's love is the force, that keeps hope alive.

Her journey, though winding, is clear in one notion,
It's paved with pure, undying devotion.

In the vast expanse of time,
moments flicker and wane,
Yet a mother's love,
forever does remain.

Not in days or years,
or the time that she takes,
But in countless moments,
and the sacrifices she makes.

From sleepless nights,
to endless days,
Her love shines brightly,
in countless ways.
She might give up dreams,
for her child's delight,
Embrace shadows,
so they can have light.

Each choice she makes,
each step she treads,
Is for her children's future,
where she silently threads.

Even when weary,
her spirit doesn't break,
For her love's depth is measured,
in the sacrifices she'd make.

In the heartbeats and whispers,
in the stories she'd weave,
Is a testament of love,
and the legacy she'd leave.

In the dance of life, we sway and spin,
Through highs and lows, loss and win.
Yet, not in the stumble, or the fall we face,
But in our rise, we find our grace.

Life's trials, like storms, will come and go,
Yet it's our response that truly does show.
Not the weight of the trial, but our stand so bold,
Defines our story, the tale that's told.

For in the heart of challenge, amidst despair's throes,
Emerges strength, as resilience grows.
In every battle, in shadows we trod,
We define ourselves, against every odd.

As night recedes, giving way to the morn,
A new day's birth, resilience reborn.
With every sunrise, hues of gold and blue,
A testament stands, to the strength in you.

Life's challenges, like night's dark embrace,
Fade with time, at dawn's gentle grace.
For every new day, in its glow and brilliance,
Speaks of our spirit, our unwavering resilience.

Purpose, not a title, nor a gleaming badge,
It's the spark in the heart, that you can't camouflage.
Not in ranks or roles, or in accolades so bright,
But in the lives we touch, and the wrongs we right.

From the smile we bring, to the hope we instill,
Our purpose flourishes, it's a passionate will.
In the kindness we share, in the love we spread,
We find our calling, where our hearts are led.

Through trials and errors, through mists and haze,
The path to purpose, in mysterious ways.
Yet, it's there in the whispers, in the hands we clutch,
Our purpose thrives, in the lives we touch.

In the heart of a caregiver, a fortress resides,
Strength of a warrior, where compassion abides.
With hands that heal, and eyes that see,
The pain, the strife, the patient's plea.

With every touch, and every soothing word,
A battle is fought, a victory conferred.
They stand on the frontline, where emotions swell,
A warrior's heart, in empathy's spell.

Their armor is love, their weapon is care,
Fighting life's battles, with a grace so rare.
In the still of the night, or the chaos of day,
Their strength perseveres, never led astray.

Through tears and smiles, through hope and fear,
They stand unwavering, always near.
For in the heart of a caregiver, so pure and clear,
Lies the strength of a warrior, a love so dear.

REFLECTIONS
REMINISCING

In the vast orchestra, where life's melodies play,
A mother's encouragement lights the way.
Not in loud clashes, nor in roaring sound,
But in harmonious notes, love is found.

It's the lullaby sung, the tales shared at night,
The push and the pull, setting dreams alight.
In her laughter and tears, in lessons she wrote,
In the symphony of life, she's the harmonious note.

In the pages of time, under the sun's golden rays,
The bond of a mother and son always stays.
It's not just in words, or in gestures grand,
But in quiet moments, where they understand.

In shared secrets, in the glow of the moon,
In lessons taught, in tunes softly croon.
Every laughter, every tear, every joy and fear,
Writes a chapter, in their story, dear.

In the highs and lows, in challenges met,
Their bond strengthens, no regret.
For the story of a mother and son, pure and true,
Is written in moments, both old and new.

Every stutter, every pause,
A challenge faced, without applause.
Yet, each stammer, each broken sound,
Was a step towards the voice I found.
Not in perfection, but persistence I thrived,
In the struggle, my true voice arrived.
Every stutter was a step towards finding my voice.

With every obstacle, every towering wall,
With every stumble, every slip and fall,
There's a signal unseen, a nudge unheard,
A gentle whisper, an encouraging word.

It's there in the shadows, in the corners of your
mind,
A voice that assures, "You've got this, just unwind."
In the trials, in the tribulations you face,
In the challenges that seem a never-ending maze,
It's the spirit within, the strength that persists,
The unspoken courage that always exists.

With every challenge, you're never amiss,
For within you whispers, 'You've got this.'

In life's vast hallways, its unpredictable sweep,
My mother stood firm, her lessons so deep.
Teaching with love, guiding with care,
In every challenge, she was always there.

Not just to dictate, but to inspire,
To fuel every dream, every desire.
In the classroom of life, a bond so sincere,
My mother was my compass, always near.

Both teacher and cheerleader, standing tall,
Guiding me through life's every rise and fall.

Hand in hand, we tread the way,
Through sunshine bright and skies of gray.
Each lesson shared, each story told,
Shapes the future, makes me bold.

The steps with her, both fast and slow,
Teach me where and how to go.
For every journey, every milestone known,
Echoes the path we've together sown.

The steps we take together, carved in stone,
Shape the path I walk alone.

Journeying far and wide, beyond the horizon's crest,
It's not the destinations that truly manifest.
It's the laughter shared, the moments small,
The unplanned detours, memories that enthrall.

Every step, every mile, a story unfolds,
In the canvas of travel, our tales are bold.
It's not just the landmarks or places we stay,
But the imprint of memories, that won't decay.

Travel isn't just about the land or the bay,
It's about the stories we write along the way.

Amidst towering buildings, in the city's vast sprawl,
Beyond its hustle, its fast-paced drawl,
We sought and found, spaces that sing,
Moments that to our hearts, forever cling.

In quiet alleys, and bustling squares,
In the gaze of strangers, in shared wares.
Not in grandeur or statues tall,
But in shared stories, memories enthral.

In the city's heartbeat, its rhythm intense,
We crafted memories, breaking past the fence.
In the vast landscape, amidst the city's torrents,
We found moments that became our own monuments.

Upon life's vast stage, under spotlight's glare,
The world watching, every gaze a stare.
Yet amidst the many, one face stands clear,
A beacon of hope, wiping away each fear.

A nod, a smile, a silent cheer,
Whispers of courage, drawing near.
For every daunting challenge, every review,
There's that face in the crowd saying, "I believe in you."

Behind every feat, every bravado new,
Is the undying faith of a supportive few.

In the pit of the stomach, where nerves reside,
Butterflies flutter, they twist and collide.
Yet with a mother's touch, a calming breeze,
Those erratic flights find their moment of ease.

Her unwavering faith, her love so true,
Transforms fears, skies turning blue.
For with the strength of her belief so right,
The most nervous butterflies take the most graceful
flight.

Life's journey, a tapestry we weave,
With moments of joy, times we grieve.
Yet every step, every sight we behold,
Adds a thread, a story to be told.
Laughs and tears, memories we amass,
In the fabric of time, forever they'll last,
Every shared emotion, a stitch, a reverie.

Amidst the grandeur, the Mall stretched wide,
Monuments to history, side by side.
Yet, as we walked, it became so clear,
It wasn't the structures that drew us near.

Each step, each glance, each shared delight,
Became moments that shone so bright.
The laughter echoed, stories took form,
Amidst history, our memories were born.

In the vast expanse, with history's quilt,
It's the memories we built that stood, unwilt,
In the shadow of heroes, our tales still felt tall,
For in the heart of the National Mall, it's memories
that enthrall.

PART III: QUEST FOR IDENTITY

BONDS

SIBLINGS

Woven tales of youth, vivid and replete,
With playful days and secrets discreet.
In the fabric of memory, amidst all the threads,
Siblings stand out, forging paths ahead.

With jokes and jibes, and games so sweet,
They make the picture of childhood complete.
In this tapestry, with stories so myriad,
Siblings are the hues, vibrant and vivid.

In rooms filled with toys, under sunlit beams,
Whispers of adventures, laughter, and dreams.
From shared tales to silent mirth so visceral,
The language of siblings remains universal.

Time's river flows, ever so relentless,
Carving paths, both near and distant.
Where once stood bridges, strong and tight,
Walls rise, casting shadows, blocking light.
Yet amidst the rifts and growing spaces,
Echoes of past laughter find their places.
For even as divides may grow deep and long,
The pull of shared memories remains strong.
Time may separate, its power so grand,
But heartstrings of siblings forever stand.

Born from the same source, beneath the same sun,
Shared joys, shared tears, together we begun.
Yet as seasons change, so do we,
Paths diverge, as different as land and sea.
Same roots anchor us, firm and strong,
But the winds of time carry us along,
The enigma of siblings, ever intricate and expansive.

In hallways of the past, where memories reside,
Shared giggles and secrets, side by side.
The gentle tug of remembrances, subtle and strong,
Where sibling bonds are built, lifelong.
Through tears and mirth, through thick and thin,
Together we faced, a battle or a win.
In the echoes of laughter, vibrant and enlarged,
The bond of siblings forever is charged.

From playgrounds to amusement parks, from dusk
till dawn,
Our adventures, the lyrics to our childhood song.
Roller-skates to rollercoasters, high and low,
We wrote our tale in the memories we'd sow.
With each twist and turn, thrill and worry,
Together we scripted our unique story.

Between cities and years, memories stretch long,
Echoes of past laughter, our favorite song.
For it isn't the miles that pull hearts apart,
But moments missed, the pauses in heart.

Yet, memories sustain, keep us close at bay,
Reminding of times, of sunnier days.
Change shifts the ground, alters the view,
But in the heart, memories remain true.
For distance, in essence, is not about space,
But the time between shared embraces' grace.

Silent departures, whispered in the night,
Moments passed, out of love's sight.
For in the realm of unspoken farewells,
A heavy heart quietly dwells.

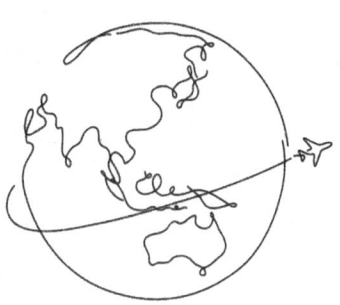

Behind walls of time, and doors once shut,
Hope persists, a feeling deep in the gut.
For even if paths once diverged, grown apart,
A key of hope can restart the heart.
Reconnecting bonds, mending the fray,
Revealing the love that never went away.

A beep, a vibration, breaking the years' quiet,
A message, a memory, rekindling an old light.
For time may pass, and silence may reign,
But memories persist, in the heart's domain.
In the simplicity of words, old bonds ignite,
Reconnecting hearts, making everything right.
For in a moment's notice, as memories unfreeze,
Siblings find the bridge across silent seas.

Though tides may push and pull us wide,
Memories anchor, by our side.
Siblings drift, yet memories bind,
A beacon of the past, we always find.

Life's vast ocean, with currents so vast,
Takes us on journeys, contrasting our past.
Yet, look to the horizon, steady and far,
It speaks of beginnings, of who we truly are.
For no matter the distance, the journey, the charted,
The horizon reminds us of where we started.
Bound by our roots, no matter the separation's size.

CHALLENGES
NEW OBSTACLES

In the quiet hallways of our mind,
Whispers of memories left behind,
Some light as feathers, free and kind,
Others heavy, to chains they bind.

There's a burden unique, distinct yet clear,
A memory's weight from a long-lost year.
Moments missed, chances not taken,
Dreams we let go, hopes forsaken.

For amid the chorus of joys we've met,
Lingers the haunting tune of regret.
Though time may move, and years progress,
It's the unsaid words that often weigh the most, no
less.

Echoes of the past, they reverberate deep,
Awakening memories, we've tried not to keep.
Among joyful tales, laughter, and song,
Are the voices of regret, telling us where we went
wrong.

Each step not taken, each word left unsaid,
Play on a loop, in the theater of our head.
The moments we let slip, the chances we didn't
seize,
Become ghostly voices, carried by the breeze.

In the vast auditorium of life's grand play,
Regret's voice often refuses to stay away.
Yet, amid this noise, let's strive to find,
The song of forgiveness, for ourselves, in our mind.

For while regret speaks, and its voice is strong,
The power to move forward is where we truly be-
long.

In the recesses of thoughts so deep,
Where fears and sorrows silently seep,
A battle rages, unseen, unknown,
A fight for clarity, a quest to be shown.

Doubts form chains, despair wears a crown,
In this inner world, it's easy to drown.
The external world sees a smile, hears a jest,
Unaware of the storm, the internal unrest.

But in these tunnels, so dark, so confined,
There's a quest, a search, for a light to find.
For even in the abyss, where shadows play,
There's a glimmer, a spark, showing the way.

Though battles are hard, and the night seems long,
In the heart of despair, there's a resilient song.
It sings of hope, of a dawn yet to come,
Urging us forward, till the battle is won.

Clouds of past trauma, and gusts of current fears,
Together they summon, a tempest of tears.
In the vast sky of our mind, stars seem to wane,
As shadows of yesterday bring forth their pain.

The horizon seems distant, the climb steep and high,
Every step forward feels like a goodbye.
To dreams once cherished, to days once bright,
As the struggle takes over, day merges with night.

But remember, in the darkest of skies,
The stars shine the brightest, a pleasant surprise.
Each one a testament, to battles once fought,
To resilience shown, to lessons hard-taught.

The promise of tomorrow is not in the clear,
But in facing the storm, confronting the fear.
For in the heart of struggle, when all seems amiss,
Lies the potential for growth, and the genesis of
bliss.

In the vast landscape of the soul,
Where emotions play their unending role,
There's a terrain, rugged and steep,
Where secrets are buried, and wounds run deep.

But to traverse this landscape, wild and vast,
We must first acknowledge our troubled past.
For in admitting pain, in voicing the cry,
We summon the strength to give healing a try.

Reaching out isn't a sign of defeat,
But a brave admission, incredibly sweet.
For in seeking help, we're not showing we're weak,
But finding the voice, the courage to speak.

The world might be loud, with its relentless din,
Yet, there's a whisper of hope from within.
By extending a hand, seeking a guide,
We begin a journey, with hope by our side.

Each step, each tear, every laugh, every plea,
Brings us closer to who we're meant to be.
For in the realm of healing, as vast as the sea,
The bravest step is to just let oneself be.

There's a maze in our mind, a labyrinth so vast,
Filled with memories of the present and the past.
At times, the path gets clouded, the way seems un-
clear,
Surrounded by walls of anxiety and fear.

Yet, in this complex maze, where darkness might
dwell,
There's a beacon of hope, a potential to quell.
For acknowledging pain, admitting the strife,
Is the first step taken to reclaim one's life.

In the vastness of struggle, it's easy to hide,
To keep emotions bottled up inside.
But the strength of a soul isn't in silence and stealth,
It's in seeking the path, the journey to mental health.

For every shadow that lurks, for every night that's
long,
There's a hand outstretched, a place to belong.
In the quest for healing, when the climb gets steep,
Remember, the first step is to let oneself weep.

In the tempest of life, where storms often brew,
With winds that are harsh and skies seldom blue,
There's an anchor that holds, a tether so dear,
A haven, a comfort, always near.

It's the warmth of a family, the embrace so true,
A bond that's unbreakable, a connection not new.
Through the highs and lows, the joy and the strife,
The family's the constant, the anchor in life.

When words fail to capture what hearts wish to say,
A simple hug conveys it in a more profound way.
For the language of love isn't bound by mere words,
It's a melody felt, a song of the birds.

In the embrace of a loved one, there's magic so pure,
A touch of the soul, a love that's secure.
It's a dance of the heart, a waltz of trust,
A symphony of feelings, loving and just.

So when life gets challenging, when times are tough,
Remember your family, their love is enough.
For in the stormy seas, when all seems forlorn,
It's the anchor of family that helps us be reborn.

In the sprawling journey of existence,
Through the maze of life's every instance,
When the path is rocky, the climb so steep,
There's a force that guides, a connection so deep.

It's the strength of family, the bonds that we share,
The love, the laughter, the way that we care.
When the world seems cold, when hope seems dim,
The warmth of family is the encouraging hymn.

When words fail, when gestures fall short,
The embrace of a loved one is the comforting port.
In the arms of family, the world fades away,
The worries, the fears, they all stray.

For the language of love isn't spoken aloud,
It's a whisper, a feeling, a connection endowed.
In the vast canvas of life, it's the colors most bright,
The family's love, the most beautiful sight.

So let's cherish the bonds, the moments we've spent,
For the love of family is life's sweetest scent.
In the dance of existence, through calm and storm's
chase,
Family's the music, the eternal embrace.

In the vast expanse of life's grand tapestry,
Where every thread weaves its own legacy,
There lie scars, both seen and concealed,
Echoing tales of battles, strength revealed.

Every scar, an emblem of battles faced,
A reminder of times, moments embraced.
They speak not of weakness, but strength anew,
For every wound tells a story that's true.

Each tear shed is not a sign of defeat,
But a testament to resilience, bitter and sweet.
For in every droplet, there's an ocean of emotion,
A saga of heartbreak, love, and devotion.

Every dawn brings a chance, a hope to renew,
To repaint our canvas with colors bold and true.
Not to rewrite history, but to start a new page,
To embrace every moment, every age.

In the storybook of existence, grand and vast,
It's not about fitting molds of the past.
But to find our own rhythm, our own unique song,
To understand where our hearts truly belong.

Because life isn't about the usual or the norm,
But about weathering every storm.
For in acceptance, we find our own space,
A journey of hope, love, and grace.

In the quiet corners of our minds,
Lie memories, both harsh and kind.
Each reflection, a piece of our soul,
A chapter in a story, making us whole.

But often, the harshest critic we meet,
Is the one staring back, in reflections discreet.
For we tally our errors, both big and small,
Forgetting our triumphs, neglecting them all.

To move forward, to truly be free,
We must let go of what used to be.
Forgive ourselves, for we're only human,
Every mistake, every forgotten plan.

For in self-forgiveness, there lies a key,
To unlock potentials, to truly be.
In the mirror of self, may we always see,
A person worthy of love, and a chance to be free.

Upon life's winding path we tread,
With hopes and dreams, both said and unsaid.
Each step, a challenge, a test of our might,
But with every stride, we chase the light.

Self-acceptance, a journey so vast,
Learning from our present, understanding our past.
For every stumble, every tear,
Is a lesson learned, conquering fear.

The path may be rocky, often so steep,
Yet, with determination, the rewards we reap.
For in accepting ourselves, flaws and all,
We stand tall, breaking every wall.

Each challenge faced, a milestone passed,
Bringing us peace, that's meant to last.
For at the journey's end, what we truly find,
Is a heart at peace, a contented mind.

SELF-DISCOVERY
COMING OUT (PART I)

In the realm of our inner world,
Where thoughts and feelings are unfurled,
Lies a path, both twisted and straight,
A journey of destiny, a dance of fate.

There are shadows, dark and deep,
Whispers of doubts that never sleep.
Yet, there's light, warm and bright,
Guiding us through the darkest night.

The echoes of fear, they try to sway,
But the voice of courage leads the way.
For in every challenge, in every strife,
Lies a lesson, a spark of life.

With each step on this intricate dance,
We learn to give ourselves a chance.
To embrace our flaws, to see our worth,
To understand our role in this vast earth.

For self-acceptance, it's not just a phase,
But a lifelong journey, an eternal maze.
Yet, with courage in heart and light in sight,
We find our true self, shining bright.

In the quiet room, where reflections stand,
A mirror holds a truth, deep and grand.
For beyond the face, beyond the skin,
Lies a soul, a spirit within.

We see our scars, our laughter lines,
Memories of old, ties that binds.
Yet, deeper still, if we dare to stare,
Lies a truth, both raw and rare.

Who are we, beneath the guise?
Beyond the mask, the compromise?
The hardest search, the toughest quest,
Is to find oneself, to truly attest.

The mirror of truth, it doesn't deceive,
It shows us all, what we believe.
Yet, to truly see, to truly know,
We must look beyond, let our true self show.

For in the depths of our very soul,
Lies a story, waiting to be told.
In the mirror of truth, may we come to see,
Our truest self, our destiny.

It starts with a whisper, a thought within,
A secret kept, a battle to begin.
Coming out, it's not just a word,
It's a path, a journey unheard.

A moment's courage, a lifetime's quest,
To be oneself, to be one's best.
It's not a statement, not a decree,
But a conversation, a way to be free.

With friends and family, with those we trust,
We open our hearts, we break the crust.
Through tears and smiles, through joy and strife,
We share our truth, we live our life.

For coming out, it's a journey divine,
A chance to be oneself, to truly shine.
It's a conversation, a lifelong embrace,
A path to love, acceptance, and grace.

In the garden of life, where friendships bloom,
There are flowers that grow, that conquer the gloom.
True friends, they stand by our side,
In joy and sorrow, with nothing to hide.

They see our heart, our essence, our soul,
They understand our dreams, our purpose, our goal.
Not bound by labels, by what we appear,
But drawn by love, by what's truly dear.

Through thick and thin, through highs and lows,
True friends are there, their support they show.
They're a treasure rare, a gem so fine,
A beacon of trust, a love divine.

For what we are, it's not just a face,
But a spirit unique, a special place.
True friends see that, they understand,
In the journey of life, they hold our hand.

A secret carried, a truth untold,
A burden heavy, a heart on hold.
The fear of judgment, a constant weight,
A locked-up feeling, a closed-up gate.

To be oneself, a simple plea,
Yet fear and judgment make it a decree.
The world may stare, the world may frown,
But the heaviest burden drags us down.

It's not the truth that weighs us sore,
But the fear of what others may have in store.
To break the shackles, to set things right,
We must face the fear and embrace the light.

In the court of opinion, a stage so vast,
Judgments are cast, shadows are cast.
But the harshest judge, the one most severe,
Is not the crowd, but our own fear.

Our mind's creation, our inner plight,
Fear judges us with all its might.
It whispers doubts, it holds us back,
It binds us tight, it veers us off track.

We must face it, we must stand tall,
For in the end, it's no judge at all.
It's but a shadow, a figment, a lie,
With courage and love, it will surely die.

The joy of friendship, the laughter shared,
A bond so unique, nothing could be compared.
But when the truth emerged, and shadows fell,
It changed our story, rang a different bell.

The cold winds of prejudice, took one away,
A heart once open, now led astray.
Yet, as one door closed, many others opened wide,
Showing the power of love, with arms held high.

Acceptance poured in, from corners near and far,
Reminding that love outshines any scar.
For every judgment, a hundred hands reached out,
A testament to kindness, without a doubt.

The world can be harsh, and some may depart,
But true human kindness, is an endless art.

Life's pathways twist and often turn,
With lessons harsh, and memories to earn.
In this intricate maze, of joy and despair,
A true friend's hand, shows that they care.

When clouds gather, and darkness looms,
When happiness fades, and sorrow consumes,
It's the touch of a friend, their guiding might,
That cuts through the gloom, bringing light.

In moments of doubt, when paths seem blurred,
A friend's voice, is the song most heard.
For in life's complex, ever-changing dance,
True friends guide us, given half a chance.

Their love is the compass, steady and true,
Guiding us forward, our whole life through.

In the quiet corners of our hearts,
Lie fears that threaten to tear us apart.
The whispers of doubt, the stares that judge,
The world that often refuses to budge.

Yet amidst these trials, a fire burns bright,
A beacon of hope, cutting through the night.
For courage isn't the silence of fears,
But the voice that rises, fighting the tears.

It's the strength to stand, when the world says fall,
The resolve to answer our innermost call.
For in the face of adversity, true valor is shown,
When we embrace our truth, make our identity
known.

In the midst of the storm, when darkness is near,
Courage is the light that makes our path clear.

The journey to self, is seldom straight,
With twists and turns, guided by fate.
A road filled with stones, shadows and strife,
Yet, every step forward, is a slice of life.

For authenticity, is not just a word,
It's the song of the heart, waiting to be heard.
The battles we face, the tears we may shed,
Are but milestones, as forward we tread.

In the eyes of the world, we may seem different,
apart,
But authenticity, is the song of the heart.
With every challenge, every tear that we dry,
We're not just surviving; we're learning to fly.

For the road may be long, and the journey may seem
steep,
But every stride taken, is a promise we keep.

To ourselves, to the world, as our story unfolds,
That we'll live our truth, brave and bold.

ACCEPTANCE
COMING OUT (PART II)

In the quiet corridors of our mind,
Where secrets lie and fears entwined,
We sometimes craft our own restraint,
From whispers of doubt, from societal taint.

Each link a fear, each clasp a dread,
Chains we carry, by which we're led.
The burden of 'should', the weight of 'must',
Holds us back, in these chains we trust.

Yet, within us, a strength does lie,
To break these chains, to reach the sky.
For the heaviest weights, we come to see,
Are not of metal, but of self-decree.

When we shed these bonds, embrace our true core,
The world opens up, opportunities galore.

So let not the fear, nor judgment's might,
Keep us chained, steal our light.
For self-acceptance, true and profound,
Is the key that makes freedom resound.

In life's vast expanse, amidst its grandeur and noise,
We often lose ourselves, silenced by other's voice.
The weight of expectations, society's decree,
Can cloud our vision, make us forget who we want to be.

Yet, in the quiet moments, when fear casts its shade,
A spark of courage, can light the darkest glade.
For the journey to self, though fraught with despair,
Begins with a step, a breath of fresh air.

A step into the unknown, into shadows deep,
Where fear and hope, their silent vigil keep.
Yet, with every stride, as the path unfolds,
The shadow of fear, gradually loses its hold.

And in its place, acceptance starts to grow,
A light that illuminates, a radiant glow.
For the journey may be long, the path unknown,
But self-acceptance is the seed, from which love is sown.

In the chapters of our story, where paths intertwine,
Family stands out, a beacon that will shine.
It's not just heritage, or the roots we can trace,
But the love that binds, the shared time and space.

Blood might connect us, a bond innate and true,
Yet family's heart is in the moments we accrue.
The comforting voice during midnight's despair,
The embrace that reminds us of the love always
there.

Through trials and joys, through calm and through
strife,
The essence of family is more than just life.
Not tied by mere genes or old family lore,
But by shared laughter, memories and so much
more.

In the dance of existence, with its ebb and flow sway,
Family's the rhythm that keeps the chaos at bay.
For beyond just blood, it's the bond we enhance,
With love, understanding, giving each other a
chance.

In a world filled with noise, where judgments are
passed,
We often erect shields, lest we're typecast.
Walls made of fear, doubt, and regret,
Guarding our hearts from threats and upset.

Yet, in the chill, with doubt at our rear,
There's a warmth, a solace that draws near.
The embrace of acceptance, true and profound,
That makes barriers crumble, brings lost souls
around.

Like sunshine piercing a cloudy gray morn,
Acceptance assures us, we're not forlorn.
It surrounds and uplifts, a balm for the soul,
Quieting the chaos, making us whole.

With its gentle touch, the world becomes clear,
Barriers dissolve, and we overcome fear.
Our spirit feels buoyant, our path becomes free,
For with true acceptance, we're as strong as can be.

No need for defenses, no walls, no facade,
The warmth of acceptance helps us applaud,
Our unique existence, with all its grace,
Ready to meet life, face to face.

Amidst life's vast landscape, both noisy and wide,
There are truths whispered softly, secrets confide.
In gentle nudges, or a phrase quite terse,
Life's grandest lessons, the universe's verse.

While scholars seek answers, deep in their books,
Revelations are found in simple looks.
A child's innocent query, a lover's soft sigh,
Speak volumes more than any scholarly tie.

A moment, a murmur, a sign so slight,
Yet, it lights up the dark, like the moon at night.
With weight and with wisdom, simple words unfurl,
Revealing deep truths, making clear the world.

The simplest expressions, honest and pure,
Hold power and depth, making us sure,
That wisdom isn't just in long tales spun,
But often in words, simple and one.

Gazing into the eyes that have seen us evolve,
Witnessed our rises, and watched us dissolve.
In the look of a loved one, without guile or art,
We find a clear image, the essence of our heart.

Not the face in the mirror, staring stoic and still,
But the reflection in eyes that have climbed every hill.
With us through triumphs, by our side in defeat,
Showing us ourselves, making our picture complete.

In laughter shared, in tears wiped away,
In silent moments, at the break of day.
In the care, in the concern, in the joy, in the strife,
Through loved ones, we truly perceive our life.

They hold up a mirror, devoid of pretense,
Revealing our essence, our core, our sense.
For through their eyes, without bias or shelves,
We get the rare chance, to truly see ourselves.

The flaws, the beauty, the depth and the lore,
All that we are, and hints of what's more.
In the gaze of our kin, both familiar and elves,
We find the purest reflection of ourselves.

A lie may offer a moment's respite,
But truth, in the end, always shines bright.
For in honest admissions, in vulnerable states,
The bond grows strong, love resonates.

The fortress of trust, with bricks of truth laid,
Can withstand storms, is never easily swayed.
Where honesty thrives, connections run deep,
Promises made are promises to keep.

Though the truth can be hard, sometimes even grim,
With it, real connections aren't just a whim.
For when honesty reigns and pretense does end,
The bond between hearts, time cannot rend.

Deep bonds are formed, both old and new.
Through laughter that echoes, secrets whispered low,
Connections are nurtured, relationships grow.

A chuckle shared, over tales of old,
Or secrets exchanged, stories boldly told.
Acceptance, unspoken, in gestures so slight,
Bring souls closer, in the softest moonlight.

The moments of mirth, the times of despair,
The silent nods, the empathetic care.
These threads, so slender, yet powerful and true,
Bind hearts together, in shades of every hue.

Amidst life's cacophonies, loud and rife,
Shared moments stand out, adding color to life.
For in these shared snippets, genuine and deep,
Lies the essence of bonds, we forever wish to keep.

The tapestry of relationships, intricate and grand,
Is woven by shared moments, hand in hand.
For it's these shared instants, both big and small,
That form the essence, the core, the all.

In the dance of existence, with its myriad roles,
Comes a moment to shed, to be reborn.
To step out of shadows, to say, "This is me,"
To be out and proud, to truly be free.

No more hiding, no more fear,
Just authenticity, crystal clear.
A voice resonates, a heart takes its stand,
No longer confined, no longer banned.

Being out is like breathing air anew,
With every breath, more honest, more true.
It's living life, with no barrier or guise,
With open hearts, and truthful eyes.

No more concealing, no more pretense,
Just pure being, no need for defense.
For to live authentically is to truly be,
Yourself, unmasked, honest, and free.

he / him

she / her

they / them

When the door is opened, and we step outside,
Embracing our true selves, with nothing to hide,
Being out means more than words can convey,
It's the dawn of acceptance, the start of a new day.

The joy in being you, unfiltered, sincere,
Is a celebration of self, so crystal clear.
No more hiding in shadows, no more disguise,
Just the pleasure of living, under open skies.

The beauty of being out, being gay, bi, or more,
Is the liberation from norms, the freedom to ex-
plore.
In this world so diverse, so colorful and bright,
Being out is a triumph, a beautiful sight.

Embrace your identity, let your flag unfurl,
Show the world the true you, the genuine pearl.
For in this acceptance, in this joyous decree,
Lies a life filled with love, where you're free to be.

Let your colors shine, let your voice sing,
For being out is about embracing everything.
Your identity, your love, your spirit so strong,
In living authentically, you can't go wrong.

PART IV: REFLECTIONS AND REVELATIONS

HEARTFELT WORDS
A LETTER

In the sands of time, where footprints are laid,
Your memories are etched, never to fade.
Though waves may come, with relentless might,
Your imprint remains, a beacon of light.

The tales we shared, the laughter and tears,
Echo in my soul, transcending the years.
Though tides of life, may wash them away,
Your memory stands, unyielding, to stay.

In the depths of my heart, where love does reside,
Is a place for you, always side by side.
Even as time moves, relentless and fast,
Your footprint in my heart is built to last.

In the silence of nights, when the world stands still,
I hear your voice, a gentle thrill.
Though years have passed, since you've been gone,
The echo of your words continues on.

The melody of love, a song so sweet,
Is a tune my heart will always repeat.
For even if your voice, fades with the days,
Your love's symphony, forever plays.

In the chambers of my soul, where memories lie,
I hear our song, reaching the sky.
The notes may change, the rhythm may shift,
But the love we shared, is a timeless gift.

Every beat of my heart, every tear I shed,
Is a reminder of words, once said.
Though time may mute, the sound of your voice,
The melody of your love is my heart's choice.

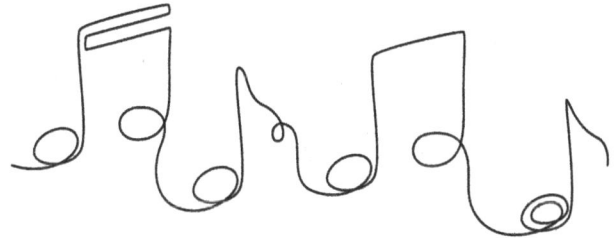

There are shadows cast, where secrets reside.
Moments of regret, whispers of despair,
Yet, love's radiant glow fills the air.

In the silent nights, when guilt takes hold,
I remember your laughter, pure and bold.
Moments of pain, they come and they go,
But love's enduring light continues to glow.

Though regrets may haunt, like specters of old,
It's love's warmth that keeps out the cold.
For in the vast expanse, of life's endless fray,
It's the love we share that lights the way.

No matter the mistakes, no matter the cost,
In the heart of love, nothing's truly lost.
For even as shadows come, fleeting and slight,
It's our shared love that brings the light.

In the pages of memories, where thoughts are
penned,
Lie words left unsaid, messages unsend.
Heavy they weigh, like stones on my soul,
Yet love's silent language makes me whole.

The glint in your eye, the curve of your smile,
Told tales of love, mile after mile.
Though words were lost, in the whirlwind of time,
Love's melody played, a silent chime.

In the caverns of regret, where shadows play,
The language of love lights the way.
For even in silence, hearts understand,
The unspoken bond, the invisible hand.

Though words were missed, and some left to chance,
Love spoke in gestures, in every glance.
For love transcends, time's relentless trot,
Speaking in ways, words simply cannot.

In the grand tale of existence, where time takes its
toll,
It's not the years we count, but the stories retold.
For the true worth of a life, rich and profound,
Is found in the hearts, where love was unbound.

Whispers of deeds, echoes of grace,
It's not time, but impact, that leaves a trace.
For in the vast cosmos, endless and wide,
It's the hearts touched that matter, not the ride.

Glimmers of kindness, gestures so sweet,
Moments of love, memories replete.
For a life's true measure, profound and great,
Is the difference made, regardless of fate.

Whispers of moments, fragments of time,
Shared laughter, shared tears, in life's prime.
For it's not just tales, written or told,
But the lives touched, the hands we'd hold.

Glowing with hope, burning so bright,
In the darkest nights, being the light.
For a legacy's worth, more than gold,
Is the hope instilled, the futures we mold.

In the journey of life, with its highs and its bend,
It's not just the start, or the eventual end.
For the legacy we weave, precious and thrilled,
Is about love shared, and the hope instilled.

Though hands can't touch, and eyes can't meet,
The heart feels a rhythm, a pulse, a beat.
For love knows no bounds, no barriers to face,
It's eternal, undying, transcending time and space.

In the quiet of night, when stars softly gleam,
Love's bond persists, like a never-ending dream.
Though worlds apart, or so it might seem,
The bond of love remains, a luminous beam.

For in life's grand theater, with its joy and its strife,
Physical presence may fade, such is the nature of
life.
Yet one truth remains, amidst loss and gain,
The bond of love endures, through sunshine and
rain.

In nature's embrace, where secrets reside,
The echoes of loved ones, forever abide.
With each whispered breeze, with each leaf's gentle
sway,
Their presence is felt, in a profound way.

The rustling of leaves, the songbirds' sweet tune,
Speak of loved ones, under the moon.
In every soft shadow, in daylight's warm glow,
Their essence remains, this we surely know.

In moments of stillness, when the world's noise does
cease,
Their memory lingers, bringing comfort and peace.
Though physically absent, in spirit, they stay,
Guiding, protecting, showing the way.

For in the vast cosmos, with its wonders unknown,
Through silent whispers, love's presence is shown.
In the heart's quiet chambers, memories are drawn,
Reminding us always, loved ones are never truly
gone.

Beneath the veil of fleeting time,
Where memories echo and chimes align,
Gratitude stands, firm and true,
A bridge that colors both the old and new.

Past moments, like golden grains of sand,
Slip gently through the hourglass in our hand.
Yet with gratitude's touch, they glisten and gleam,
Woven into the fabric of our present dream.

Memories, once scattered, now find a place,
United by hope in a heartfelt embrace.
For it's gratitude's song, melodious and clear,
That reminds us of love, ever near.

As we journey forward, facing unknowns untold,
Gratitude's bridge offers promises to uphold.
Connecting past joys, to hopes that await,
It's the love that shapes our ever-evolving fate.

When shadows fall, and darkness creeps,
And the world in silence weeps,
There emerges, against the pitch-black sky,
Stars of hope, love, and gratitude, shining high.

Loss may shroud us in its cold embrace,
Leaving voids that seem hard to erase.
Yet, amidst this obsidian night, so vast,
The luminescence of love is unsurpassed.

For each twinkle, each glimmering light,
Is a testament to love's undying might.
Hope, like a beacon, pierces through,
Guiding us with a vision anew.

So, when the night seems endless and deep,
Remember the promises these stars keep.
For even in the profoundest, darkest phase,
Love, hope, and gratitude set the sky ablaze.

LOOKING BACK
GOING BACK

In the soil of our birth,
Roots run deep, anchoring our worth.
Yet as time marches, unswayed, undeterred,
Our paths are by choices and experiences stirred.

From the seeds of the past, sprout stories anew,
Crafted by challenges, dreams we pursue.
For while beginnings have a familiar song,
It's the journey's melody where our souls belong.

Echoes of yesterdays, in memory's halls,
Whisper lessons, as the present calls.
While the past holds tales, lessons to glean,
It's the present's stage where life's act is seen.

We glance back, not to linger or stay,
But to learn, and then find our way.
For the gift of now, vibrant and tense,
Is the canvas of life, the essence of present.

The compass of our past, in hand,
Guides us through memory's land.
Not to dwell or answers seek,
But to gain perspective, unique.

Each glance back, a lesson learned,
Every page, a memory earned.
For in reflection, we find direction,
A clearer path, a deeper connection.

Whispered words, silent tales,
Hidden trails where memory sails.
Unspoken chapters, veiled in mist,
Yet their impact, we can't resist.

Like a compass, they guide our core,
Though some stories we might ignore.
For in the silence, truth unfolds,
And it's these tales that make us bold.

Blood may bind, but love runs deeper,
Embracing in the darkest hour, as a keeper.
In joy and sorrow, true family stands,
Holding you close with steadfast hands.

Through tears and smiles, thick and thin,
They're the anchor, the constant spin.
Not just by blood, but by heart's decree,
Family is who chooses to stand by thee.

Four walls make a house, but love makes it more,
A sanctuary where emotions freely pour.
A haven of memories, both old and new,
Home is the feeling, pure and true.

With every heartbeat, in every nook,
It's more than a place, it's the love you took.
It's the solace in chaos, the light in the night,
Home is where the heart feels just right.

Paths twist and turn, as lives drift apart,
Yet the heart's compass, it never does start.
For those once cherished, wishes remain,
May love and joy forever be their gain.

Though journeys change, one truth stands clear,
The hope for their happiness is always near.
For in the heart's deepest, silent chant,
Wishes for their well-being never slant.

When our heart's content, it freely gives,
Wishing joy, for as long as one lives.
For in every kind thought, every silent prayer,
Reflects a heart at peace, beyond compare.

May others find joy, happiness start,
For such wishes mirror a contented heart.

Crossroads and junctures, decisions we face,
Guided by instincts, sometimes a trace.
Each choice a step, in life's grand dance,
Embracing our path, giving life a chance.

With gratitude in heart, conviction in stride,
Contentment finds us, by our side.

Through memories' lens, the past may glow,
Echoes of what was, a familiar show.
Yet ahead lies a path, wide and bright,
With promises untold, and dreams alight.

For each step forward, potential anew,
The future's embrace, ever true.

CLOSING THOUGHTS
EPILOGUE

In the fabric of life, each thread is unique,
Some are born of chance, others we seek.
Yet, genes alone, a family can't create,
It's love and care that determines our fate.

Bound not by birth, but by hearts that care,
It's the love we give, the moments we share.

By blood, we are connected, a lineage so vast,
A history that's shared, a tie to the past.
Yet true kinship goes beyond mere genes,
It's carved in loyalty, in behind-the-scenes.

Through thick and thin, in joy and in strife,
Family stands by, the anchor of life.
In love and loyalty, the bonds grow strong,
With them, we find where we truly belong.

Numbers may count, in many a tale,
But love's strength, it never grows stale.
When hearts unite, and spirits entwine,
That's when families truly shine.

Bound not by count, but depth of heart,
Family's strength is a work of art.

Storms will rage, winds will blow,
Yet amidst it all, family's glow does show.
Their support unwavering, steadfast, and true,
Guiding us through shades of blue.

In turbulent tides and roaring gales,
It's family's anchor that always prevails.

Though blood may bind with ties so tight,
True families glow with love's pure light.
Acceptance deep, and understanding clear,
Makes every voice a joy to hear.

Bound by heart, not just by birth,
A family's love proves its worth.

Each one distinct, a melody of their own,
Yet together, a harmonious tone is shown.
From highs and lows, to in-between,
Their collective song is rarely seen.

A dance of notes, so free and spry,
Creating the family's lullaby.

In the vast tapestry of existence,
Some threads shine with a unique persistence.
Not by birth, but by choice they intertwine,
Signifying a bond, pure and divine.

They come as strangers, stay as true kin,
Through thick and thin, in loss and win.
The gratitude for such souls runs deep,
For they're the promises life chose to keep.

Beyond blood, beyond mere name,
Their presence turns life's tide, never the same.
Such blessings rare, we hold them near,
For in their love, all becomes clear.

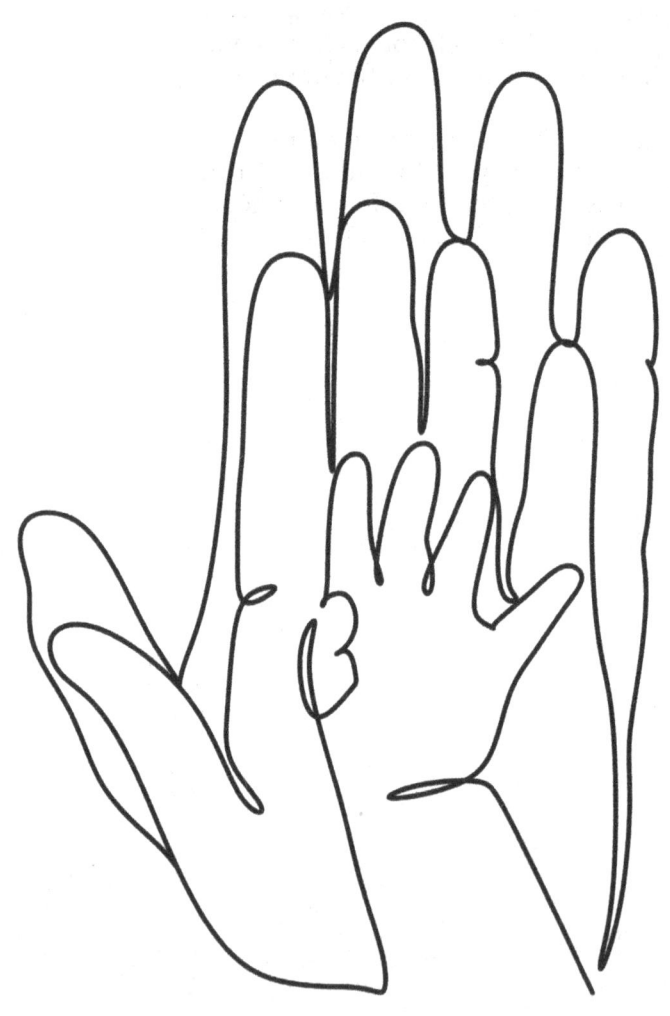

Family is where our stories start,
Where love, undying, plays its part.
Each chapter written, each memory spun,
Underneath the same nurturing sun.

Bloodlines can be deep, traditions old,
But family's essence isn't always told.
By who stood at your birth or by your side,
But by those whose love never did subside.

For family extends beyond mere blood's bond,
Reaching further, far and beyond.
To the ones who stood by, through thick and thin,
Whose presence felt like a win.

Those who held your hand through darkest night,
Who became your strength, your guiding light.
Through joyous feasts, heartaches, and strife,
They've been the consistent rhythm of your life.

It's not just about shared histories or a common past,
But about bonds built to forever last.
Whether through birth or by choice's decree,
They're the roots and branches of your tree.

Embracing you for who you are, with love so grand,
Supporting, understanding, always there to stand.
So, when life's melodies take twists and bends,
Know with true family, the love never ends.

WHISPERS OF HOPE: POETIC REFLECTIONS ON FAMILY AND LIFE

AFTERWORD

As the pages of this book come to a close, my journey continues to unfold with new chapters and adventures. Since the time of writing "Wishes of Love," life has presented me with a myriad of opportunities and challenges, each shaping me into the person I am today.

Graduating with a Bachelor's degree in computer engineering was a significant milestone, a testament to years of hard work, dedication, and an insatiable thirst for knowledge. But the academic journey didn't end there. I've embarked on a new academic pursuit, diving into the intricate world of cybersecurity with a Master's program at the esteemed Johns Hopkins University. The digital realm is vast and ever-evolving, and I'm excited to be at the forefront of protecting and navigating it.

Professionally, my journey took an exciting turn when I joined DoubleVerify as an intern in the summer of 2022. The experience was transformative, and by November of the same year, I was honored to be brought on board as a full-time CorpIT Engineer. The dynamic environment and the brilliant minds I work with have been instrumental in my growth.

Outside the confines of work and study, I've channeled my passion for technology and creativity into developing two full-fledged apps, now available on the Apple App Store.

These apps are a reflection of my commitment to innovation and my desire to contribute positively to the digital ecosystem.

While this book captures the essence of my memoir through poems, I'm thrilled to share that an expanded version of "Wishes of Love" is on the horizon. This edition will delve deeper, offering a more detailed exploration of my life's journey. For those who've walked with me through the pages of the original memoir, this upcoming version promises a richer, more immersive experience.

Life is a continuous journey of learning, growing, and evolving. As I look to the future, I'm filled with gratitude for the past and excitement for what lies ahead. Thank you for being a part of my story, and I hope you'll continue to join me in the chapters yet to be written.

Warmly,
Liam Sawyer

ABOUT THE AUTHOR

Liam Sawyer, born on February 5th in the pictur-
esque landscapes of Ukraine, embarked on a trans-
formative journey at the tender age of five. Along-
side his sister, Caitlyn, he was adopted into a world
of boundless love and opportunities. Today, he calls
Staten Island, NY, his home, where he cherishes
every moment with his mother, June, and his loyal
canine companion, Deacon.

With a natural inclination towards technology, Liam
pursued his passion and graduated with a Bachelor's
degree in Computer Engineering. He now navigates
the bustling streets of New York City as an IT Engi-
neer, leaving an indelible mark in the tech world.

Though Spain might seem like a distant memory,
Liam's love for travel remains undiminished. Each
journey he undertakes adds a new chapter to his
ever-evolving story.

OTHER BOOKS WRITTEN BY LIAM SAWYER

- *Wishes Of Love: A Memoir Of Love, Hope, And Family*